Pray and Learn Letters with

Edgar G. Frog
on
Alphabet Mountain

Written and Illustrated By -
Linda D. Washington
Edited By – Rita K. Jeffries

Copyright ©2024 Products and Activities for Christian Education (PACE)

A PRAYER FOR THE CHILDREN

Father,

You sent Your only begotten Son, Jesus, to show us Your Love. Thank You for loving us so much. We know that those who believe Jesus, are forgiven of all their sins. And because You and Jesus forgave us, you told us to forgive everyone that does something bad to us. Father, we ask that You please help everyone to FORGIVE others. We know that You do not want anyone to be hurt. So we ask that You put Your love in our hearts to always pray and obey You—to truly know You!

Thank You Father!
In Jesus name we pray!
Amen

Dedicated to:
Herbert Washington Jr.
and
Gregory Nichols

Story Introduction

Edgar G was a boy who liked to pray with his parents every day. They taught him about God's love. Edgar G learned that God his Father in heaven, Jesus, and Holy Spirit loves him and everyone. His mom and dad told Edgar G to ALWAYS PRAY and talk to God about everything. But sometimes Edgar G would forget to pray.

At school, Edgar G would play and have fun with his friends. One day he went to school just like he always did. But this day he did not want to listen to his teacher. So, he sat down on the floor, closed his eyes very tight and thought about being in a far-away land where he could hop and play all day.

When he opened his eyes, he was no longer an Edgar G boy. He was an Edgar G Frog. . . AND that wasn't all his problems, he was no longer at school, he was lost. Now he was trying to get home, but a great big mountain was blocking his way. Edgar G must figure out a way to climb ...

Alphabet Mountain

"Wow!"
said Edgar G, as he stared at the big mountain in front of him.
"How do I climb this?"

Looking up, he could not see the top of the mountain.
The mountain extended up, *into the clouds*.

Edgar G shouted," **CAN ANYBODY TELL ME ABOUT THIS MOUNTAIN?"**

No one answered.

He yelled again,
**"IS ANYONE HERE?
CAN ANYBODY TELL ME ABOUT THIS BIG OLD TALL MOUNTAIN?"**

From the side of the mountain came this rustling, crinkle crackling noise.

Edgar G listened.

Crinkle Crackle. **Crinkle Crackle. Crinkle Crackle**.
The sound got closer and closer, louder and louder.

Crinkle Crackle. Crinkle Crackle.
Edgar G backed up.

The noise got closer.
CRINKLE CRACKLE

Edgar G shivered.

The noise got louder.
CRINKLE CRACKLE

Edgar G froze.

Just when he thought that there was absolutely no place to run …

A raccoon jumped up from underneath a pile of sticks and screamed,

BOO!

Edgar G was so frightened that he leaped up
and almost ran *straight* into the mountainside.

Edgar G's voice trembled as he said,
**"You scared me.
Why did you scare me?"**

"Wanted to!" the raccoon quickly answered.
"I can do anything that I want to do," said the raccoon.

"Anything?" questioned Edgar G.

"That's what I said----and I bet I can scare you again," the raccoon replied.

"Oh no you can't," Edgar G stammered.

The raccoon yelled, "I'll prove it!"
He ran right past Edgar G.

"Oh my,"
Edgar G sighed as he slowly sank down to the ground.

"I don't like that raccoon.
He thinks that he can run around and scare me
and do anything he wants to do.
He's not very nice.
He's a pest. And I don't like him."

Edgar G leaped to his feet and said,
"I don't care what he does next.
I can hop.
I can run.
I can leap.
I can skip.
I can even walk backwards.
Yes, I can!
I can beat that old raccoon at anything."

"Just let him try something. I'll karate chop him.
Yeah, that's what I'll do.
Just like this……**Ahhhhhh HA!**"

Edgar G yelled out as he jumped sideways into the air.

Edgar G thought about how he used to play in the sand at school.

He could dig the deepest holes.
He would dig so deep that his teacher would smile and place DANGER signs near the holes he dug.

He missed his teacher, his parents and his friends.
He wanted to go home.

But first he had to take care of that pesky raccoon.

**"I know!
I'll set a trap for him.
He thinks he can scare me... Ha! I'll show him."**

Edgar looked around for something that he could use to dig a hole, but he didn't see anything.

Edgar G used his hands and dug the deepest and best hole that he had ever dug.

He looked around to see if the raccoon had returned but did not see him.

Edgar G was ready to put his plan into action.

He asked himself, **"What is my plan?**

Let me think.

I can trick that raccoon and make him fall into this hole. Hmm....maybe I could call him and make a funny face at him. Then he'd run towards me *real fast* and just as he gets near me, Smack!"

Edgar smiled as he clapped his hands together to make a smacking sound.

**"I'll step aside real fast. Then down he'll go into the hole.
Yes! That's my plan.
I'll trick him real good.
Yes, I will.
I'm Edgar G! You can't trick me!"**

Edgar G's thoughts were interrupted by sounds near the mountain.

The raccoon ran out from behind a rock.
He once again had Edgar G's attention.
Edgar G watched as the raccoon stopped directly in front of the hole.

The raccoon began to sing.
(to the tune of Twinkle, Twinkle Little Star)

Alphabet Mountain, Up So High
With Letters Up into The Sky
Find The Letters in Your Name
It Will Help You Play the Game
Alphabet Mountain Up So High
With Letters Up into The Sky

"**Is that Alphabet Mountain?**" Edgar G asked pointing up.

It sure is! replied the raccoon.

Edgar G asked, **"What do I have to do to climb it?"**

The racoon said, **"To climb that mountain, you must know the alphabet."**

Edgar G said, *"the alphabet?"*

The racoon said, **"Yes, the alphabet!
The letters in your name are part of the alphabet."**

Edgar G closed his eyes to think.

He said, **"My name is Edgar G.
Edgar G, that is all that I know.
I don't know all my alphabet.
I don't know all my letters.
I didn't listen when my parents and teacher told me about the letters in my name.
But I remember they told me to *always pray*."**

The raccoon moved towards Edgar G.

Without thinking Edgar G hopped backwards *away* from the raccoon, And....

Ker-Plop!
Down Edgar G fell
into the biggest and deepest hole that he had ever dug.

"WHOA!"
screamed Edgar G,
as he slid down, down, down and into his own tricky trap.
"This hole wasn't for me.
It was for *YOU!*
I wanted to trick you because I thought that you were mean!"

The raccoon looked into the hole and said,

"I'm not mean. Why would you say that I'm mean?"

"You frightened me, Edgar G said.
I didn't like it when you yelled BOO to me."

"I was only trying to play with you," the Racoon said.
"I really shouldn't do everything that I want to."
"I'm sorry," said the raccoon.
"WILL YOU FORGIVE ME?"

Edgar G said, **"Hmm, I don't know.
I need to pray.
My mom and dad told me to *Always Pray and Trust God*!"**

Edgar G knew that heavenly Father would help him choose the right thing.

So Edgar G prayed:

**"Father,
I know you love me, and I love you.
Mommy and daddy told me to always talk with you about everything.
So here I am again.
Will you help me to forgive this racoon for scaring me?
Thank you, Father!
Amen"**

Edgar G looked up at the raccoon and said,

**"I FORGIVE YOU FOR SCARING ME.
And I'm sorry for trying to trick you into falling into this hole.
I thank God that no one got hurt."**

Edgar G knew that God loves everyone.
God told us to forgive others;
And the raccoon had asked Edgar G to forgive him.
So, Edgar G forgave him!

Edgar G extended his frog hand up from the hole saying,
"My name is Edgar G. Can we be friends?"

The raccoon answered, **"My name is Rascal Raccoon. "**
"Yes! we can be friends."

Then Rascal Raccoon pulled his friend, Edgar G frog,

UP

and out of the hole.

Rascal Raccoon said, **"Friends help each other.
Let me help you climb that mountain."**

Edgar G asked,
**"How?
How can you help me?
I don't know all my alphabet.
I don't even know the first letter in my name."**

**"Pray and Think Edgar G.
Remember you said to Always Pray,"** said Rascal Raccoon.

Again, Edgar G bowed his head and prayed:

**"Father,
I remember that You sent Jesus and told us,
You would never leave us.
I trust You!
I know that Jesus and Holy Spirit are with me.
So Father, will You, Jesus and Holy Spirit help us
to climb this mountain safely
and remember the letters we learned?
Thank You Father!
I love You!
Amen"**

When Edgar G finished praying,
he looked at the letters on the mountain.

He said, "Ed.....gar.... Ed....E...E,,,E!

That's it!

The first letter in my name is E!
**Thank You Father!
Thank You Jesus!
Thank You Holy Spirit!
You helped me to remember."**

Edgar G hopped over to Alphabet Mountain with Rascal Racoon.
And together they found the first letter in Edgar G's name.

Edgar G shouted E as he hopped onto his first mountain letter.

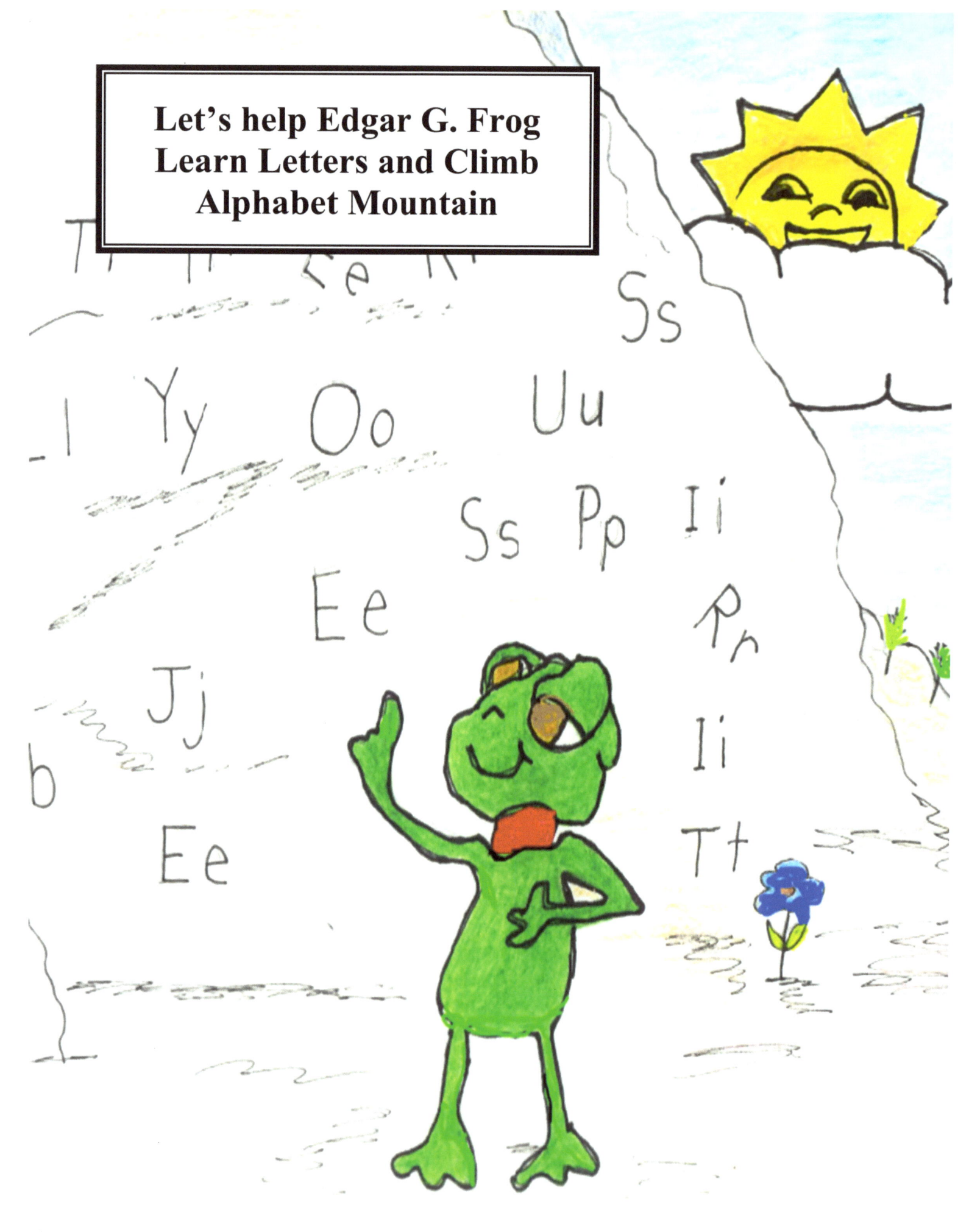

Memory Verses to Teach Children

Forgive others for the things they do wrong, then your Father in heaven will also forgive you for the things you do wrong. But if you don't forgive others, then your Father in heaven will not forgive the wrong things you do.

Matthew 6:14-15

Pray Always!

1 Thessalonians 5:17

Love one another like Jesus loves you.
That is what Jesus told us to do.
John 13:34-35

"Friend of Jesus" Song to Teach Children

(to the tune of Bingo)
I have a friend who loves me BIG!
And Jesus is his name.
He told me to love others BIG
To love them just the same.

J…E…S…U…S
J…E…S…U…S
J…E…S…U…S

And Jesus is his name.

Alphabet Mountain
Pray and Learn Letters
Game Instructions

Before beginning the game, carefully cut out the Edgar G Frog game pieces; the game cards; and game sheet at the back of this book. To stand the game piece up after cutting fold it on the crease.

1) AT THE BEGINNING OF THE GAME SAY:
God wants us to PRAY AT ALL TIMES!
We can pray and talk to God about anything.
Let's pray before we play.

2) LET EACH CHILD WHO WANTS TO PRAY DO SO.
If no one chooses to pray, an adult (as an example) can say a brief prayer to our heavenly Father and end the prayer by thanking Father. (Remind the children who prayed to thank God after they pray)

TO PLAY ALPHABET MOUNAIN
Number of Players: 2

3) DECIDE WHO WANTS TO PLAY FIRST AND SECOND.
Choose a colored Edgar G. Frog game piece and place on the game sheet by the feet of Edgar G Frog.

4) MIX THE CARDS
Place the cards in a stack with the frog-side face down within reach of both players.

5) EACH PLAYER, WHEN IT IS THEIR TURN
a. Pull the top card.
b. Hop their playing piece the number of frogs on the card. (Each card has 1, 2, or 3 hops)
c. Name each letter that the player passes, up to (and including) the space they land on.
IF THE PLAYER DOES NOT RECOGNIZE THE LETTER YET, THEY CAN ASK SOMEONE WHO KNOWS.

6) WINNING THE GAME
Climbing Alphabet Mountain is achieved by pulling a card that would take the player beyond the last letter.

7) IF ALL CARDS ARE USED AND THE PLAYERS HAVE NOT REACHED THE FINISH LINE
Mix the cards and stack them. Then use the cards over again.

Playing Pieces

Cut the playing pieces along the color lines to separate them.
After the four playing pieces are separated, fold the bottom of the playing piece along the white dotted line to stand the piece up on the game sheet.
Extra playing pieces are included.
Option: Use different objects as playing pieces, such as a button and a rock, etc.

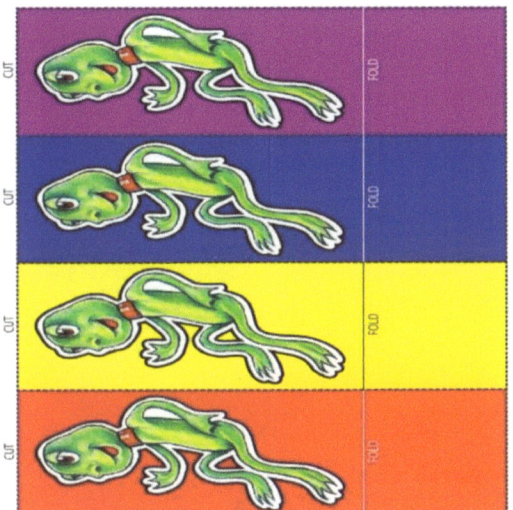 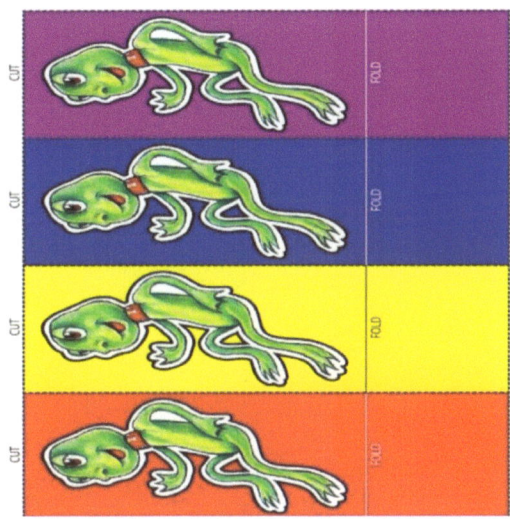

Recommended: After cutting to separate the playing pieces, keep all of the game parts, which includes, the playing pieces, cards and game sheet in a zip lock type bag,

 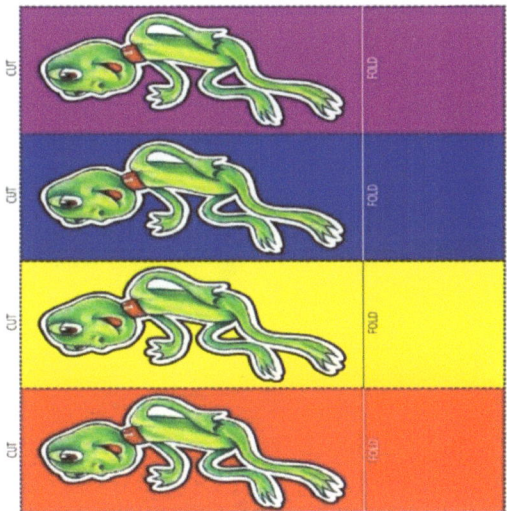

GAME CARDS
Sheet 1 of 2
Cut cards out along the lines

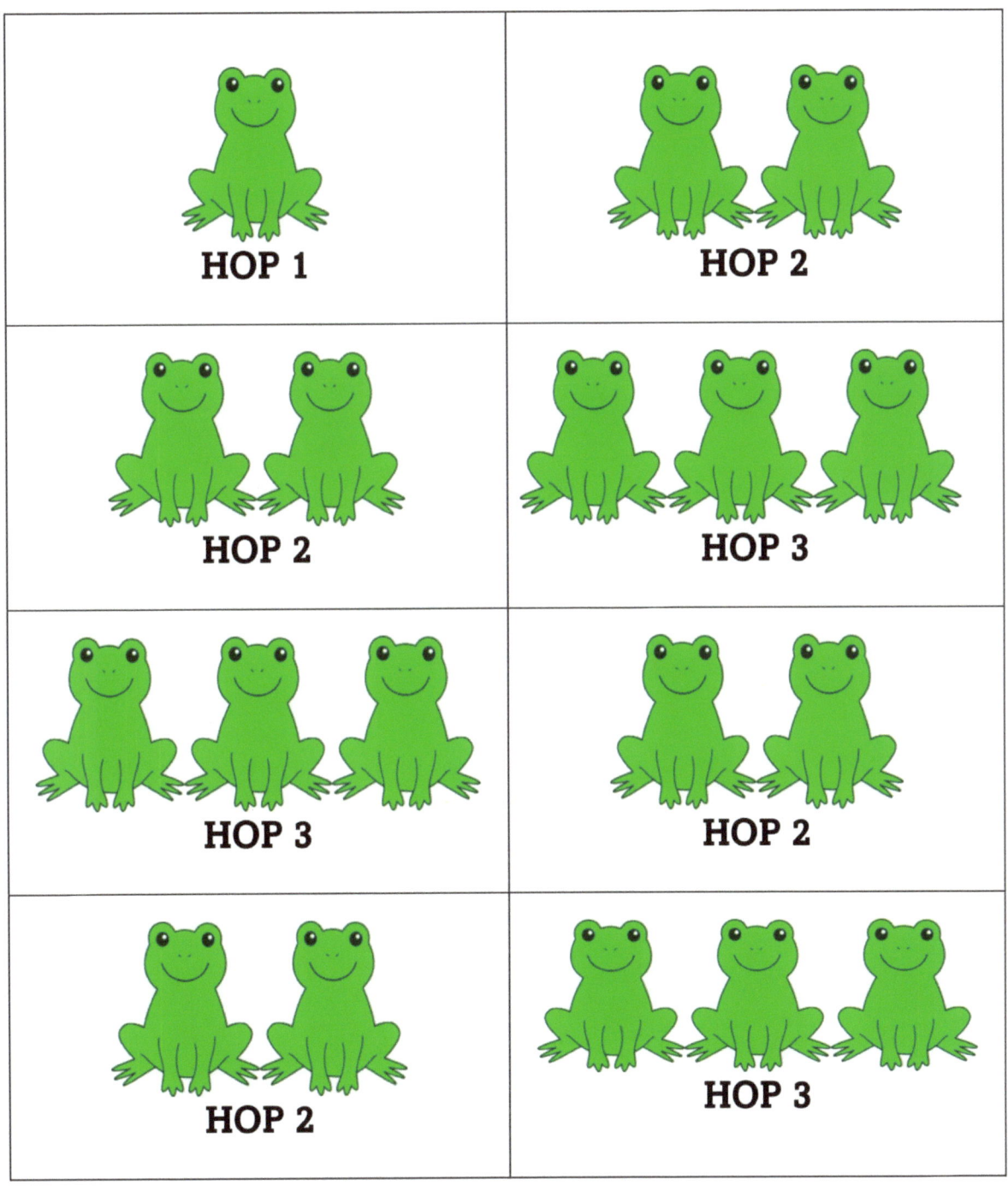

GAME CARDS
Sheet 2 of 2
Cut cards out along the lines

HOP 1	HOP 1
HOP 2	HOP 3
HOP 2	HOP 1
HOP 1	HOP 1

Alphabet Mountain
Game Sheet

Cut Here

Z z Y y X x
S s T t U u V v W w
R r Q q P p O o N n M m
F f G g H h I i J j K k L l
E e D d C c B b A a

Begin

1

www.ingramcontent.com/pod-product-compliance
Lightning Source LLC
Chambersburg PA
CBHW041535040426

42446CB00002B/102